YOUR KNOWLEDGE HAS VALUE

- We will publish your bachelor's and master's thesis, essays and papers

- Your own eBook and book - sold worldwide in all relevant shops

- Earn money with each sale

Upload your text at www.GRIN.com and publish for free

Bibliographic information published by the German National Library:

The German National Library lists this publication in the National Bibliography; detailed bibliographic data are available on the Internet at http://dnb.dnb.de .

Imprint:

Copyright © 2016 GRIN Verlag, Open Publishing GmbH
Print and binding: Books on Demand GmbH, Norderstedt Germany
ISBN: 9783668464995

This book at GRIN:

http://www.grin.com/en/e-book/368975/review-of-english-with-an-accent-language-ideology-and-discrimination

Laura Götz

Review of "English with an Accent: Language, Ideology, and Discrimination in the United States" by Lippi-Green

GRIN Publishing

GRIN - Your knowledge has value

Since its foundation in 1998, GRIN has specialized in publishing academic texts by students, college teachers and other academics as e-book and printed book. The website www.grin.com is an ideal platform for presenting term papers, final papers, scientific essays, dissertations and specialist books.

Visit us on the internet:

http://www.grin.com/

http://www.facebook.com/grincom

http://www.twitter.com/grin_com

Universität Potsdam

Philosophische Fakultät

Institut für Anglistik/Amerikanistik

Linguistik

WiSe 2015/16

Modularbeit – Review

Lippi-Green, R. (2012). *English with an Accent: Language, Ideology, and Discrimination in the United States* (2nded.). London: Routledge.

Eingereicht von:

Laura Götz (2. Semester. M.Ed. Englisch/Französisch.)

Contents

INTRODUCTION

English with an Accent (short EWA; 2012) is Rosina Lippi-Green's updated and expanded second edition of the 1997 version on standard language ideologies and the perception of accents. Over eleven years she has enlarged the associated online biography with more than 800 sources, from newspaper articles to government documents (p.xxii). As a result, "pretty much every sentence in EWA had to be rewritten, every source checked, reevaluated, replaced or brought up to date, and every conclusion challenged" (p.xxii). Each chapter is indeed extensively enriched by multiple well researched and emphasizing sources, suggestions for further reading, and discussion questions for the classroom.

One of the strengths of this new edition is definitely the profound and deep research of sources and Lippi-Green's engagement therewith. Questioning the readers' well-kept beliefs about language seems to be one of the author's intentions. She shows that no matter what education one has received, which age, gender or race an individual belongs to, no one is free from standard language ideology (SLI). Lippi-Green's careful study of numerous samples of interviews, advertisement, popular culture and media round up to a very understandable and reliable piece of work. It even creates the effect of linguistic awareness in daily non-linguistic life as language is being deconstructed to its simplest forms and, subsequently, its reconstruction explained in meticulous detail. That way, linguistic elements that trigger discrimination against speakers, who deviate from SLI, are dismantled and this gives the reader a chance for personal reflection.

The book's insights on language discrimination and social repercussions are vividly described. That results in a captivating but also pensive reading experience. Interestingly, the author addresses scholars as well as non-linguist laypersons and asks them to be objective about language in order to have them distinguish between the general beliefs about language and linguistic facts. She argues that the beliefs people have accepted as truth about accent and language emphasize and justify social inequalities (p.xx).

SUMMARY

Chapters 1 – 6

For reasons of facilitation this review will summarize chapters according to their broad fields of topic and not one by one. The beginning chapters (1-6) can be condensed as an act of deconstructing the conceptual layers that underlie the dissemination of language myths and the power of standard language ideologies. Taking her time do so, Lippi-Green provokes a thorough engagement of the readers into the issues and, additionally, draws on their personal experiences with language by blending in examples of American pop culture (i.e., p.17). The author calls the first chapter "the Linguistic facts of life" and sums up five facts being relevant to the book's claim: all spoken language changes over time; all spoken languages are equal in terms of linguistic potential; grammaticality and communicative effectiveness are distinct and independent issues; written language and spoken language are fundamentally different; variation is intrinsic to all spoken language, and is mostly symbolic (adapted from pp.6-7). Instead of dispelling language myths for the general readership, EWA examines these myths in the focus of social inequality.

The following chapter "Language in motion" takes up the final myth regarding regional variation, which was discussed beforehand, and will be an essential parameter throughout the book. With a focus on the subsequent chapters, Lippi-Green also introduces relevant cases of variation in the United States in detail. This includes the presence or absence of (r) in syllable codas; the Northern Cities Chain Shift; lexical variation and discourse markers; weak and strong verbs (p.27). With this chapter, the author introduces the coactions of social and linguistic factors and reasons that American dialects do not necessarily die out but are constantly in motion. Furthermore, she establishes that "variation is an intrinsic and functional feature of the spoken language" (p.40) and discusses why varieties are labeled according to their differences to each other (i.e., substandard) and what the corresponding consequences thereof are. Moreover, this chapter gives an example of the monograph's accessibility to readers without a linguistics background. Lippi-Green achieves this by giving helpful support such as spelling out the IPA (International Phonetic Alphabet), incorporating findings of pioneering studies (i.e., Labov, 1962), or taking the reader on appealing imaginary analogies (p.48).

Taking up the book's title, Lippi-Green then delves into "The myth of non-accent" (chapter 3). She starts out by explaining the function of myth and how it can be used to influence people's behavior. According to those findings, the author reasons why a "standard language" is a myth. In this chapter, she establishes the basic notion thereof because, in the following, she moves into the discussion of the conceptual heart of the book: Standard Language Ideology (SLI). Chapter three positively scintillates with the analogy of a Sound House (p.48) which describes how our accents develop while, at the same time, considering the adoption of new ones or the abandon of old ones. Lippi-Green builds those metaphors up in a chronological way covering moments in a time span from birth up to adulthood. By means of architectural images, a fictive protagonist's accent development and potential "renovations" on her Sound House, or in other words phonology, are described. All those changes are made in order to assimilate or discern her Sound House from the ones people around her have built. The author underlines that accents in every language will naturally change over time and that myth and ideology in these changes are powerful features.

The following chapter ("The standard language myth") aims at answering the question who has language authority by exploring the role of lexicographers and the decision of which "standard" enters dictionaries. Lippi-Green continues her discussion of language myths by disassembling the belief of the existence of a standard variety of language and is, therewith, showing who could misuse this belief and who benefits from it. The author warns that, if a "standard" were established by an elite group, "there [would be] nothing objective about this practice" (p.58). Dictionaries are widely consulted as authority over daily questions about language. Therefore, deciding to analyze the effect and consequences of dictionaries is an appealing move by the author. That is how she successfully directs attention toward the propagation of SLI.

Lippi-Green's conceptual core work begins after the preparatory stages in chapter five, which looks into the process of "Language subordination" (p.66), and more precisely, how discrimination of people works through SLI. Certainly, standard language ideologies have been well established ever since and, thus, many have fallen for following it. However, the author also examines how language subordination works and proposes the analytical tool of "The language subordination model" (p.70) to present how standard language ideologies are distributed and, more importantly, why people consent to the stigmatized social position SLIs impose on them. Several processes are included by the model: language is mystified; authority is claimed; misinformation is generated; targeted languages are trivialized; conformers are held up as positive examples; non-conformers are vilified or marginalized; explicit promises are made; threats are made (p.70). In varying detail, Lippi-Green comes back to those processes and gives examples in the course of the book. In general, social implications of why people are asked to speak a certain language or with a certain accent are discussed in this chapter.

Although the functioning and reason of language subordination is not researched in its entirety yet, the author provides a possible approach thereof: "The educational system: fixing the message in stone" (chapter 6) claims that SLI is at first introduced and enforced in schools, no matter how well-trained or -intentioned the teachers are. The author successfully points out the gap between policy and practice in schools by arguing that although the policies which recognize linguistic diversity have been long established over 40 years ago, little has been done yet to implement these.

Chapters 7-18

The following chapters will be summarized in this review as Lippi-Green gives examples of the concept of language subordination which is set out above and, hence, strengthens its credibility, reliability, and authenticity. Her examples show how SLIs affected and still affects speakers of different languages and varieties of English in the U.S. negatively. While discussing this, the English speakers with their language background (i.e., ch. 7, 9, 14, 15, 17) and home regions (i.e., ch. 7, 8, 11, 12) stay in the foreground. For each of the cases she discusses how SLI has a direct impact on belonging, may it be real or imagined, and portrays the availability of opportunity in the American context. To give an example, chapter 11 deals with speakers in "The Southern Trough" (p.217) and talks about the linguistic perceptions of and by them. The author is interested in topics such as accent reduction, identity, resistance, and the trivialization of southern varieties of English and their speakers. Linking into other chapters of this book (i.e., ch. 9, 12), Lippi-Green points out a crucial aspect in SLI: if one wants be successful in America, it is commonly assumed that there is no way around assimilating one's speech through accent reduction. In a similar manner, the chapter "The real trouble with Black language" (p.182) emphasizes that AAVE (African American Vernacular English) has historically developed around the question of who has the right to be an authentic American. What is more, this chapter sketches the main facts about AAVE grammar, corresponding controversies around this variety and conflicting viewpoints towards it coming from African American as well as Anglo American communities. Additionally, the later chapter 16 ("Case Study 1: moral panic in Oakland") puts the Oakland Ebonics Controversy from the 1990's in the spotlight and contributes an even closer look at some immediate consequences of SLI in the African American community. Further examples of ethnic minorities' in the United States and their varieties of English are provided in the newly added chapters 14/15 of this second edition (see back of book). Those two chapters focus on Latinos and Asian Americans portraying simultaneously the experiences made by them as minorities as well as the attitudes of SLI defenders toward them.

Like a red thread Lippi-Green lets the role of English speakers of different linguistic backgrounds and home regions in the context of language subordination reoccur over several chapters in EWA. This following paragraph will now refer to chapter seven which questions the innocence of cartoons in terms of manipulating a standard language ideology. Through analysis of Disney animated films the author presents incredible data on racial stereotyping and lays open the problem of trivializing cultures and characters. Based on her enlarged resources, the author added 14 more movies to her data pool (p.112), this second edition of EWA reveals that the heroes of children's movies speak with a variety that is widely understood as "Standard American English" (SAE). In stark contrast stand the language varieties used by the villains and animals: varieties of ethnic minorities in the U.S. With eye-opening examples, Lippi-Green portrays the traits attributed to characters according to their language. The author claims that convivial individuals tend to speak with an Italian accent, irresponsible characters can be easily portrayed as irresponsible, and animals or the "smart-mouthed, lazy, disrespectful" ones speak often AAVE (p.119). Here, the interplay of linguistic and non-linguistic features, such as race, is underlined once more by Lippi-Green and stands as a representative model for the non-fictional world. Moreover, as "children are not passive vessels who sit in front of the television and let stories float by them" (p.104), the author points out that by watching Disney movies, children are easily socialized into prejudices. Race certainly is one of the topics that arise continuously throughout the chapters (cf. ch. 17), and the Disney example is definitely one of them.

Furthermore, Lippi-Green looks into SLI present in politics and media (chapter 8: "The information industry"). Here, she examines the connection between political figures and the communication industry. She specifically addresses how opinions and attitudes about the way politicians speak, rather than what their contents try to convey, disseminate through media and, thus, have the power to influence the public's perception on the speaker. Another case of language subordination is given in the following chapter when language becomes crucial in the intersection of success and failure at the workplace as well as the power distribution, or the lack thereof, of the judicial system. Basing the drawn conclusions on real cases, this chapter portrays authentically the difficulty of prosecuting employers after discrimination took place at the workplace, in particular, when policies were agreed upon to protect people from it. A similar argument is given in the context of housing for the case study at the end of the book (ch. 17).

The concluding chapter summarizes the findings of the previously given cases of discrimination against speakers of accented English. By maintaining and adhering to a standard language ideology, those speakers of a different variety are automatically subordinated. The author draws hereby on her original premise that speech is judged not on the contents but on the quality of the said (p.335).

EVALUATION

Theoretical position of the author

After extensive and well-grounded research on different forms of subordination of speech and its perception by others, Lippi-Green claims that no one is free from standard language ideology (SLI). No matter what education one has received, which age, gender or race an individual belongs to, she gives a new appearance to the notion of having an accent and, therefore, raises and challenges every readers' linguistic awareness in daily life. The arguments for that assertion are grounded in an American context as the nation founded by immigrants embodies like few others the coexistence of languages and, thus, accents of English.

Points of critique

EWA presents the school as the social organization exposing children to SLI for the first time (p. 73). Unfortunately, it leaves out the role that caregivers, teaching staff, and lastly, parents play, who are legally bound to educate their children. That role is usually paired with an ideological socializing function and should, hence, be taken under more scrutiny.

Moreover, the language subordination model is too multifaceted and too complex on many levels, that it might complicate matters instead of facilitating them. Although Lippi-Green usually rendered her contents accessible to a general audience, this model seems to act in an opposite way. It could be ameliorated by focusing on fewer variables.

Compliments

Despite the mere concentration on the U.S. the study does not become unreliable but rather benefits from it as data is nonetheless plentifully refurbished. Focusing on an American context, preconditions for an accent study seem ideal because of the intermingling of different

8

languages, and corresponding dialects, in history and present. That, in return, allows to draw conclusions of various other linguistic situations all over the world.

Lippi-Green's monograph is special because readers do not necessarily have to have a linguistics background in order to understand the contents; the author manages to have the accessibility of the contents complement their complexity. She does so by providing easy support such as spelling out the IPA, simplifying complex concepts by playing with analogies (i.e., pp.1-4; p.48 "The Sound House"), or incorporating key concepts and results of studies (i.e., Labov, 1962). So the reading provides a guide through the sometimes mysterious linguistic jungle and, simultaneously, wins with its rather narrative and capturing writing style. Thus, EWA has great capacities to attract a general audience.

Despite the linguistic focus, EWA broaches many controversial topics and challenging contents also applicable to a social studies or even law background. For that reason, the monograph serves as fuel for debates in school or university classes alike and therefore furnishes useful material for teachers or university professors. Moreover, a large range of discussion questions and classroom exercises as well as suggested further reading or references to the interactive companion website help to teach seeing the bigger picture not only in scholarly disciplines but also in real life experiences.

CONCLUSION

Coming back to the very outset of Lippi-Green's monograph, she centralizes the controversy of language subordination and standard language ideologies. According to the thorough argumentation, this premise seems coherent. Nevertheless, while reading, the awareness of how deeply ingrained SLI in fact is sets in. That revelation of being instilled into standard language ideologies could have the strength to make readers feel uncomfortable as they, hence, inadvertently promote it, although some might even strive for language equality. Ultimately, the author calls for a shift in the way people think about language and, particularly, how those paradigms affect the way people think and behave towards each other. With that in mind, it is difficult to ignore the issues raised by EWA in a quotidian life; the diversity of examples looking at different accents, background stories, or realms of real life affect every reader to some extent and is, therefore, applicable to many countries, social situations and personal beliefs.

Word count: 2842

YOUR KNOWLEDGE HAS VALUE